# RUKHSATI

*A fortune, a gift, a tear!*

By Dr Mona Aeysha Khalid

# Acknowledgement

I am thankful to Pakistan where I was born for providing me such an environment of discrimination and violence and for the custom-rukhsati that has inspired me so much that I could not stop myself to write on it.

Thanks

# Table of contents

# Introduction

In some of the societies of our world, 'culture' word is very much misinterpreted and misunderstood. Although it is a broad term, but it does not mean we should misuse its meanings and manipulate it in such a way that some of us suffer badly and become mentally sick.

Values, beliefs, traditions, and ethic are sometimes very much confusing while people follow them blindly believing them being part of their culture. Some of them are so much critical that they create different types of discrimination based on gender, race, color, ethnicity and religion.

Values and related beliefs lead us towards prejudice, discrimination and stereotyping. We all are prejudice minded and discriminate to some extent in one way or the other. Being stereotyped is not a negative trait but a fact, whereas being prejudiced means being unjust. A prejudice minded person could or could not discriminate. The best practice is not to discriminate, but it is simply not possible for human beings to become totally unbiased in all matters. We have different religions, races, colors, nationalities and ethnic backgrounds with various and countless traditions and values around us. So we behave in a certain way to keep our unique identity and feel esteemed.

In some Asian countries like Pakistan, Bangladesh and India, many beliefs about women are tolerated and accepted widely by people as a part of culture, whereas they create a huge environment of discrimination between women and men. For example, it is said, "Girls are guests in their parents' home and they are bringing them up for their (girls) future husbands or in-laws". Someone says, "This is not your house; your real house is where your future husband is living".  On the arrival of a baby-girl, mostly women proclaim, "We wish you had a baby boy so that you become powerful and honorable in society". And it is also a widely accepted belief, "Women have to face all brutalities and tortures if they want to keep their marriage" (divorced woman is always stigmatized and blamed for).

A large number of rights are presumed only for boys and girls are exempted from it based on gender only. Many jobs are thought suitable only for boys, not for girls. Girls are supposed to do many things (of minor nature) such as cleaning, doing dishes, cooking and taking care of other male members at home and boys are supposed to do many things (of major nature) such as shopping, driving, and taking part in big decisions. Such divisions of work at home basically create a huge environment of discrimination based on gender among society members that ultimately put women members at high risk.

Discrimination may cause many kinds of psychological and mental health problems for women as they could feel low self-esteem, loss of concentration, disordered vision, false self-concept, hallucinations, and memory loss. They are also at high risk to develop any kinds of personality disorders due to severe discrimination against them.

To summarize, we need to answer such questions as follows:

1. Should we not stop beliefs/traditions that generate discrimination against women?
2. Who will decide about what to do in this regard?
3. How can we end/stop unnecessary discrimination between men and women?

My proposal is that women must be surveyed for discrimination thoroughly and the results must be taken seriously by higher authorities. Then laws developed by such organizations should control the situation. Moreover, in this process of elimination of beliefs, customs, and traditions, media can play a significant role. For example: T.V. Dramas, movies, and stage shows displaying discrimination must be banned, whereas new, original, and modern themes should be introduced so that people do not follow thoughts/ roles of discrimination rather learn how to be unbiased, and equal in identity and honor.

Though the picture of women portrayed in this book is not very much identical to some women from educated families, but here I am more concerned about the general, average and below average class of Pakistan that is in deep pain indeed. They need your attention, care, love and empathy to feel themselves as a respectable and worthy human.

Thanks

Dr Mona

# Rukhsati – What Is This?

After discovering all the basic needs of children, I came to know that after food and shelter, love and a complete sense of security are the basic needs of everybody and the most essential for the little ones. Unfortunately, these little ones include girls too!

Girls of Pakistan are not burned/buried alive at all. They are born in a secure society where everyone would like to keep them with love and kindness. Before marriage they live with their parents and after marriage, they live with their husbands Parents. It is true for more than 90 % of families. Sometimes a girl lives only with her husband when in-laws fortunately don't like to see the couple out of hatred and enmity!

To make it more clear and understood fully, I can quote the words of one of my clients as she said, "I remember when I came to know myself as a girl, my identity was described as a guest in my parent's home. I used to cry like hell almost every day for about two to three hours for the fact that I would be leaving my loving parents one day! I prayed several times a day and requested God to not let me leave my home. I begged His mercy and asked for help in despair, but there was no sound to console me!"

In Pakistan, we have many traditions that we keep in the name of religion and culture, we do not care whether they bring any benefit to society or damage the personalities at large. We never mind in keeping them preserved and honor them through a blind adaptation while living in a fools paradise.

One of these so-called traditions is "Rukhsati" which means, "leaving a parental home for the groom forever". It is very well known tradition of Pakistan (I am not going into the history of this tradition). On the marriage day, the bride is supposed to leave her parents home forever as she is going to see her new home that will remain her real home until her death. Such feelings you can very easily sense through any movie songs on 'rukhsati'.  When a girl is born, people pray, "May God bless her with good luck", which means good home (of future husband).  A baby girl is never thought as a gift of God rather a responsibility from God to bring her up for her future husband /in-laws. Such feelings have been transferred from one generation to another successfully for thousands of years with no regret and guilt.

Nobody cares if a child is ready to take such a grief in her heart. A baby girl should enjoy the same quality of love, peace and security as a baby boy. She should not feel a feeling of lack,  for being a guest in her own home, with the uncertain future. She must not have a guilt of being a burden upon her parents for being a baby girl. She is too tiny to have the fear of future luck, the fear of leaving love (of parents), the fear of leaving a secure place, the fear of being homeless in the future, and the fear of living with strangers willingly or unwillingly.

Even in the most modern societies of Pakistan, 'Rukhsati' is not only observed rather manipulated in its real sense. Most of the in-laws never allow their girl-in-law to visit her parents' home occasionally or often. It sometimes becomes a big reason for divorce. Some girls take it for granted. They think they have to leave their parents' home one day for sure and there is no harm in it. They leave their parents for goodness and accept it as a norm of their society and think they should obey it blindly. Some of them visit their parents (after marriage) quite often, but they are always treated as a guest and would never be welcomed to stay forever (even in the worst circumstances).

As a result, young girls feel low in self-esteem compared to their counterparts (boys). They demand less from their parents and are thankful to them more than their siblings (boys). They try to make their parents happier than boys due to their short term stay with them. On the contrary, in some houses, they are being pampered too, but the reason is the same – Rukhsati.

In the teen years, mostly girls prefer thinking about their future husband more than their parents as they are going to leave their parent's home forever. They start dreaming about their future luck (husband, his family, his status, his habits, his education, his profession, his attitude, his personality, his belongings, etc.) that is never in their hands. So resultantly, their progress in class suffers a lot. Meanwhile, some of them are usually engaged in the family and others start worshiping actors, singers, heroes, and models.

In the late teens, mostly girls, are married and have already left their parental homes. Others are engaged. The remaining are usually thought to leave their parents' home soon in future. Otherwise, they would feel a great amount of guilt for not leaving their parents' home in time. Irrespective of the fact that both boys and girls should be brought up with the same amount of love and care, girls do not feel secure in any stage of life. Their parents love for them is limited to only some period (until they get married).

Some girls continue with the tradition happily and luckily get the luck in their life. Most of the girls miss their parent's home a lot and could not dare to come back due to societal pressures and traditional family repute. They convince themselves to stay unhappy in their husband's house (usually in-laws house) rather than going back to their parent's house. In addition, many in-laws or husbands exploit their weakness (that they do not have a place to stand) in different matters.

The girls who step ahead and come back to their parents, usually face many challenges: bhabi's (brother's wife) taunts, relatives abuses, and friends cutting remarks. In the end, many decide to return to their husband's home. Even in the hell like husbands home, girls are not ready to come back to face the societal pressures and family's disrespect.

Although, one can argue that girls can live on their own, but, for the Pakistani particular society, it is again a matter of safety, a matter of honor and a matter of repute. Therefore, no one dares to do it and no one is allowed to do it too. Here it is important to note that in Pakistan, the government is not responsible for food, education and shelter, to to be provided to its citizens. And moreover, the security situation is too bad for girls, to live alone in any streets of Pakistan.

To conclude, it is suffice to say that 'Rukhsati' is not only a tradition rather a belief that causes a girl to feel like a burden, even in her own home. It is not the tradition, rather a lifestyle that causes our girls feel homeless, home sick and guilty while sitting in their parents' laps. It is not only a custom, rather a torture that a girl faces throughout her life and never be able to get rid of it!

# Reflections Of Women Of Pakistan

'Rukhsati' is not the only thing that causes women cry from time to time. There are several other things in this regard. In Pakistan women are not allowed to ride a bicycle or motorbike since their childhood till old age. One of my clients once recalled, "In my childhood, I was not allowed to go out even to play in a park. The people around me explained me the rule that all this stuff (walking, jumping, enjoying rides in parks in free time) was not good for girls (of any age group). At that time I wished I were a boy! Later on I came to know about other things which were not suitable for girls!"

There are several other factors that create discrimination against women like choice of living alone, choice of a partner, choice of profession, choice of subjects to study, choice of dress, choice of music, and many other kinds of likes and dislikes. Moreover, there are several traditions made by men to make women feel inferior, sex objects, weak, and ultimately more vulnerable to diseases, disorders, and traumas.

In Pakistan, women are thought as men's responsibility. In other words, they are married and given to men's custody. Now it is their luck how their husbands behave and what they offer to them. Usually women are expected to do house chores perfectly and be master in cooking. One of my clients expressed her views in these words, "There was something I used to hate for my self-Cooking! So many years of my teenage passed over while thinking about cooking. So many nights gone weeping and praying for a life without cooking. The fear was developed like a phobia in my thoughts (Here it is important to note that cooking stands for long hours cooking – about 6 to 7 hours a day, for in-laws and husband by force under a set criteria while following a strict routine). She added, "I remember cutting remarks of people around me: What is the use of your good grades in exams, in the end you have to take care of your family and do the cooking!, you should be perfect in your cooking only, as this is the right way to make your man happy, very unlucky is a man who will find you as you don't know the a,b,c, of cooking at all, nobody will marry you because you cannot cook so well and many others alike carrying the same message" Then she continued, "I started fighting with me and taught me the value of cooking forcibly. I was successful to some extent, but it was just occasional relief. My mind was never at rest. I was never acknowledged as a human being! In one way or the other, my identity was linked to my father's or my husband's identity. That was not acceptable to me at that time frame at least".

In Pakistani society, mostly social gatherings and parties are arranged in such a way where girls can display themselves to make others notice them as a girl! So the ability to do a good dance is very much appreciated, especially by young boys. Dance is also very much appreciated in Indian and Pakistani movies that motivates young girls to learn it and compete. It is depicted as an essential part of love and sex life in most of the romantic movies. Other than the fact whether it is true or not in reality, many young girls start competing their selves with the heroins/models of movies and as a result they put their selves in the vicious cycle of comparing and despairing.

As one of my clients felt, "I started learning dance by imitating movie songs and following each and every step of the heroine. In spite of securing top grades in the classroom, my self-esteem was suffering  a lot due to lack of ability in dance! This was the time when I felt a strong clash in my brain between what people were expecting from me as a female in a traditional society of Pakistan and what I wanted to become like a man. The conflicts in my mind could not be resolved so easily                                     ".

What to talk about sexual education! In Pakistan, girls are not supposed to ask any question about sex from anybody including their parents. Many would argue when they get married, they would come to know what sex is. What could be the devastating side effects of ignorance of sex education, parents never pay attention to.

Mothers are very much ignorant of the basic developmental needs of their children about safety and health education. Usually they follow traditional beliefs blindly in matters related to the nourishment of their children. Mostly prefer their 'totka'(home-made remedy based on no fact) to doctor's prescription.

On the basis of the data from 1000 Pakistani women (aged 18 to 25), many (90%) said that they did not know anything about sex, 80% said that they didn't know the importance of foreplay in sex, 76% agreed that they could not talk about family planning with their future husband, 95% said that they had no right to say no to their partner asking for sex, 96% said that they didn't know anything about male capacity/ability of sex, 87 % said that they did not know about male or female's sexual problems (basic) at all , 81% said that they didn't know what is climax stage in sex for women and 99% said they had no idea what anal sex is. 80% of mothers simply did not know the importance of breastfeeding and 75% said that they had started weaning from two months on. Mostly fathers were simply ignorant of the basics of 'health and safety issues for mothers and children'.

It is not something to ignore anymore. Men try to exploit women based on their lack of knowledge about sex and life in general. Even if the male partner is not exploiting, he is ignorant of women's needs (in sex, in pregnancy, after having a baby, at home). As a result, after marriage, most women become victim of abuse of many kinds and vulnerable to many psychological, physical, and social problems. Although in some cases, women are well acknowledged/informed about all this stuff, yet they are not ready to bring any change, being used to their abused life style! Or it is too late to mend!

# Discrimination Against Women Of Pakistan

Can a girl think of her self-esteem in the conservative and male dominated society of Pakistan? Definitely not. In my research work, during Ph.D, I have observed girls' self-esteem being extremely low, was not as high as boys' self-esteem. The reason for that is not very simple rather a complex and critical combination of factors. Among those several causal factors, we will discuss only a few in this book for better recognition and clarity purposes.

Since the day a baby-girl is conceived and mother-to-be comes to know that the fetus is a female child (usually doctors hide it deliberately), the child is not so much needed. The future mother becomes sad on her luck and anxious about the child's destiny and the future ahead. The reasons for such feeling include:

- Women in general do not enjoy a secure and happy life.
- Men dominate over almost all fields of life and are considered the head of the family to take decisions and to bring fate to their family members.
- A woman with a son is considered more secure than a woman alone or with a daughter. A son is thought as a sign of pride and honor as compared to a daughter.

So the mother-to-be starts perceiving low self-esteem due to her unborn female child that would ultimately affect her child in a negative way.

If circumstances do not push her to abort the child, and the child is born, people come and wish her in the words: 'May God bless the child with male siblings in the future', 'may God bestow her great luck with loving and caring husband and in-laws', and even this 'may Load forgive the parents for the sins that caused them to have a baby-girl'. The baby girl is always given dolls to play with exclusively. If she has other male siblings, she is always neglected and boys are always preferred in the matters:

- The best food/thing/gift goes to the baby-boy whether he is older or younger.
- At serving time, the male child is served first.
- At shopping time, the male child is privileged.
- While introducing children to others, the male child is introduced first.
- Little girls are not permitted to go out to play in the parks. Usually fathers go out with their sons to enjoy out-door life.
- Young girls are expected to help their mothers in doing house chores. Sometimes they are even involved in fulfilling the needs of their younger siblings (being a care taker or a nanny).
- For the education, girls are again either forbidden or go to school for a few years. In case, they continue going to school, it will be the cheapest, nearest and only for girls!

Moreover, school going girls are not very much guided, or tutored. Parents expect them to do house chores as well as do home work. Boys are exempted from this duty, at all.

- In schools and colleges, girls are advised to choose subjects like home economics, arts, history, or literature compared to science subjects that are often taken by the boys. Educated parents generally prefer their daughters to join light professions like teaching or tutoring in almost all fields of life or professions reserved for girls only. They are rarely motivated to join army, police, navy, air force, to become lawyer, engineer, or a doctor.

- The same is true with games. Girls are encouraged to take part in easier games like table tennis, badminton, hockey, and tennis compared to horse riding, swimming, boxing, karate, weightlifting, cricket, football, gymnastics, car racing, cycling, and many others. Moreover, girls are not encouraged to play with an aim seriously unlike the boys.

- In a professional life, girls are not selected for most of the posts only because of their gender. For boys, the society is open to explore and enjoy; for girls, society is a dark valley, a jungle, and a monster that restricts them to stay at home.

- Girls cannot drive bicycles, motor bikes, buses, rikshaws, trains, taxis or trucks. Though there is no law to restrict them, and a few dare to fly airplanes too, yet it is not considered as an honorable and accepted way of life for women at large. Only boys are permissible to drive what they like.

- To run a business, again boys are very much privileged and have no limit to choose from whereas women usually run beauty parlors, garments, jewelry and tailoring shops.

- After marriage, most girls are supposed to stay at home to perform household chores irrespective of their previous profession. Men believe they have enough money to support their family so the wife needs not to go out for a job or they think their wife's job is a kind of stigma on their family.

- In many families, girls are still taken, as a burden upon family as they have to leave their parents (at marriage) with a heavy dowry (another social evil).

- It looks very awkward if a son decides to live with his wife's parents. It is taken as a stigma on the family of the boy as a whole.
- To be selected for a groom, usually girls are made-up heavily to the groom's parents who has a complete right to select or reject them on the basis of their own personal criteria.
- The divorce, which is again a matter of a moment for a boy and a matter of a fortune for a girl in terms of time, money consumed in the court sessions and social torture faced by the girl and her family.
- In general, girls have no right to ask for property rights, to pursue sex education, to ask for separate accommodation (from fathers, brothers, or husbands), and to seek for their own identity as a girl in the form of keeping a name without her fathers or husbands name extension.

All of the above factors remind the girls of their feeble, less important, undesirable, and relatively low self-esteem at home, in society and in Pakistan as a whole. So much so girls are convinced to face all kinds of discriminations and deprivations while believing that they are not as capable as men in many fields of life due to their gender based characteristics and traits. Thus the factors mentioned above contribute greatly in cultivating the lowest level of self-esteem among girls of Pakistan.

However, if you think,the picture is not that much true, then go there and see yourself or just go through the page, "domestic violence in Pakistan" in Wikipedia web site. Things are, worse even in some parts of the country. 'Honor killing' is one of the examples. There are other social evils (rape, trafficking, domestic violence, acid attacks, bride burning ) in this regard, but those crimes are out of scope of this book.

# Say 'No' To 'Rukhsati'

Everybody knows about the parents' responsibilities nowadays and its importance in developing their off springs personalities into a healthy and strong generation. Islam assigns primary responsibility of bread winning to the husband as a head of the family. This obligation includes providing food, shelter, education, safety, and love (unconditional) to the family including children for unlimited time period. According to a recent survey, about half of Pakistani population belongs to females. So how can we ignore their feelings of dejection, non-acceptance, depression, discrimination and injustice! Why parents don't think that giving security and safety (forever) to their female child is one of the most important responsibilities of their parenthood!

It is carved on a girl's heart that one day she will leave her native house and will be living in her husband's house forever, even if she is beaten, stigmatized, humiliated, abused or harassed. Some educational families do not admit and proclaim the exact words, but believe in their hidden meanings and those meanings are enough to make a girl feel worse and low in self-esteem.

Now suppose parents are not giving the message of 'Rukhsti' to their girls. The possible side-effects would be like:

- Girls will be given the same love and affection as boys.
- Girls will enjoy a secure childhood like boys.
- Girls might be securely attached with one or both parents.
- Girls will perform better in schools and colleges.
- Parents will not impose their will on girls in choosing subjects, careers and life partners.
- Parents will protect girls as much as they protect boys.

- Marriage issues will not become drastic for girls; as they would still belong to a strong family and live in a secure home.

- The husband will also come to know the status of the girl- would behave and respect her being a girl.


Therefore, to feel secure, will bring lots of benefits to a female child. She will definitely enjoy the fruits of it just like boys. She will love her parents not because of 'rukhsati', rather because she is always there to feel them. She will feel secure, in peace and in harmony throughout her life. Her role as a woman will not be marginalized like before. She will no more regret on her identity as a woman. She will thank God for her life. Her feelings will bring a great sense of self esteem to her to become a successful and happy woman in life.

# Conclusive Remarks

In the culture of Pakistan and India, discrimination against women is very much practiced through lots of traditions and customs, that create an atmosphere of frustration and anger among women. Among these unnecessary traditions and customs one is the concept of 'leaving home' after marriage- Rukhsati. This is presumed that a girl's real house is where she is going to live after marriage and that is usually in-laws house or rarely husband's house. People think that for a girl, husband's or in-laws' house is a girl's permanent place to live and die even in the worst circumstances. Usually parents decide and arrange the marriage of a girl; she has no right to choose her partner herself. Even if a girl enjoys the freedom to decide about her life partner, she will have to leave her paternal home for the husband's home forever. This tradition/concept of 'Rukhsati' is being followed by more than 90 percent of families of Pakistan.

The problem starts when a girl who is about to be born, get the feelings from her mother that she is not so much expected. Mainly due to the reason that she is going to stay with her parents as a guest for a limited time. Then the girl is born and everyone in the family wishes her a good luck. Due to a large number of unsuccessful marriages and domestic abuses, people and especially parents are very much worried about their girls' future. Girls, like boys, have the right to feel secure and safe in the home of their loving parents; however, due to the custom of 'leaving home, they remain anxious and depressed for most of the time.

Often, young little angels who see their parents as a temporary gift of God, wish they were like 'boys'. They want to have their own home from the very beginning of life when they need not to be worried about anything like home, money, safety or job. Boys are thought as the permanent members of the home so they are responsible for their parent's well-being too. Otherwise girls usually try to be nicer to their parents due to the reason they are not going to stay with them for long. Meanwhile, they also face severe discrimination at home due to their meager and uncertain status in life.

Girls psychological and physical health is always at risk due to factors: their upcoming fears, insecure attachment with their parents, vague future worries, and parents' less or no involvement in their emotional and psychological growth. Mostly girls suffer from low self-esteem and torn self image. They are less confident, less motivated, less energetic, less focused, less creative and less active. They are not interested in career building activities or serious in studies as they are not sure about their future. Though some accept the fate as it is. Not all like the system and many develop a severe anger and anxiety against the custom- Rukhsati, some retaliate and fight for their rights, some surrender and go on, but almost all girls' over all self growth, self-esteem, self-worth and self-identity are always at risk that can be saved if noticed seriously by the parents and society members well in time.

Girls need to be properly educated in this regard on, how can they find the ways to get rid of the custom 'Rukhsati' forever that is based on fake and unreasonable concepts. Parents need to understand that their girls' self growth is as important as boys' self growth.They have no right to say their girls that 'one day they are going to leave them', especially when they are too young to grasp the concept fully. It is all parents' duty to make sure that their girls feel as safe and protected in their homes as boys.

Thanks

## About The Author

Mona Aeysha Khalid, PhD, is an Educational and Developmental Psychologist, have been working as a Teacher, Counselor, and Researcher in several institutes of China, Pakistan and Cambodia.

Her major areas of interest are: self-esteem, self-concept, conceptual psychology, beliefs, self psychology, preferential psychology, cultural psychology and women psychology.

You are always welcome to contact her via email:

monaaeysha@gmail.com

Tweet@ monaaeysha

Dr Mona

www.ingramcontent.com/pod-product-compliance
Lightning Source LLC
Chambersburg PA
CBHW070243290526
45789CB00004B/1743